By Donna Latham

A Winter Home

Target Skill Sequence

Scott Foresman
is an imprint of
PEARSON

The chipmunk is looking for
a bed for the winter.

Can he sleep in a den?

No, not in a den!

Can he sleep in a pond?

No, not in a pond!

Can he sleep in a nest?

No, not in a nest!

Can he sleep in the leaves?

No, the leaves are not

a good bed for the winter.

Can he sleep in an old tree?

Is an old tree a good bed?

Yes, an old tree is the spot
for a winter nap.
It is a good winter bed.